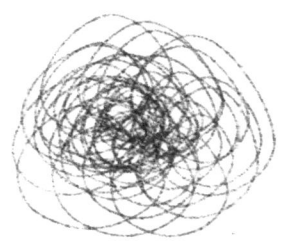

CONSIDER THIS A COZY + WARM
PLACE TO LET YOUR MIND RELAX.
MOSTLY A COLORING BOOK, BUT ALSO A LITTLE
BIT SKETCHBOOK TOO. I'VE TRIED TO INCLUDE
A LITTLE BIT OF EVERYTHING - A KITCHEN SINK IF YOU WILL.
THERE ARE SOME COLOR SPLASHES AND
TEXTURES TO INSPIRE ON SOME PAGES. BUT FEEL FREE
TO COLOR RIGHT OVER - IN FACT LAYER LAYER LAYER
THAT'S WHERE THE MAGIC IS!

BUT OF COURSE, YOU KNOW THIS.
THERE ARE NO RULES.

SHOW OFF YOUR FINISHED PIECES:
#MAKEYOURMARKCB AND REQUEST NEW
DESIGNS!

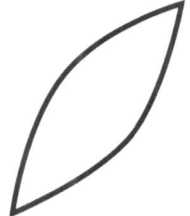

THANK YOU KINDLY FOR
CHOOSING THIS BOOK.
I'M GRATEFUL FOREVER!
LOOK FOR MORE TO COME.

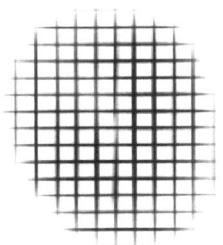

Kate Capone

KATE CAPONE
WWW.OHSOSUITE.COM
INSTA: @OHSOSUITE_STUDIO

COLOR CHART

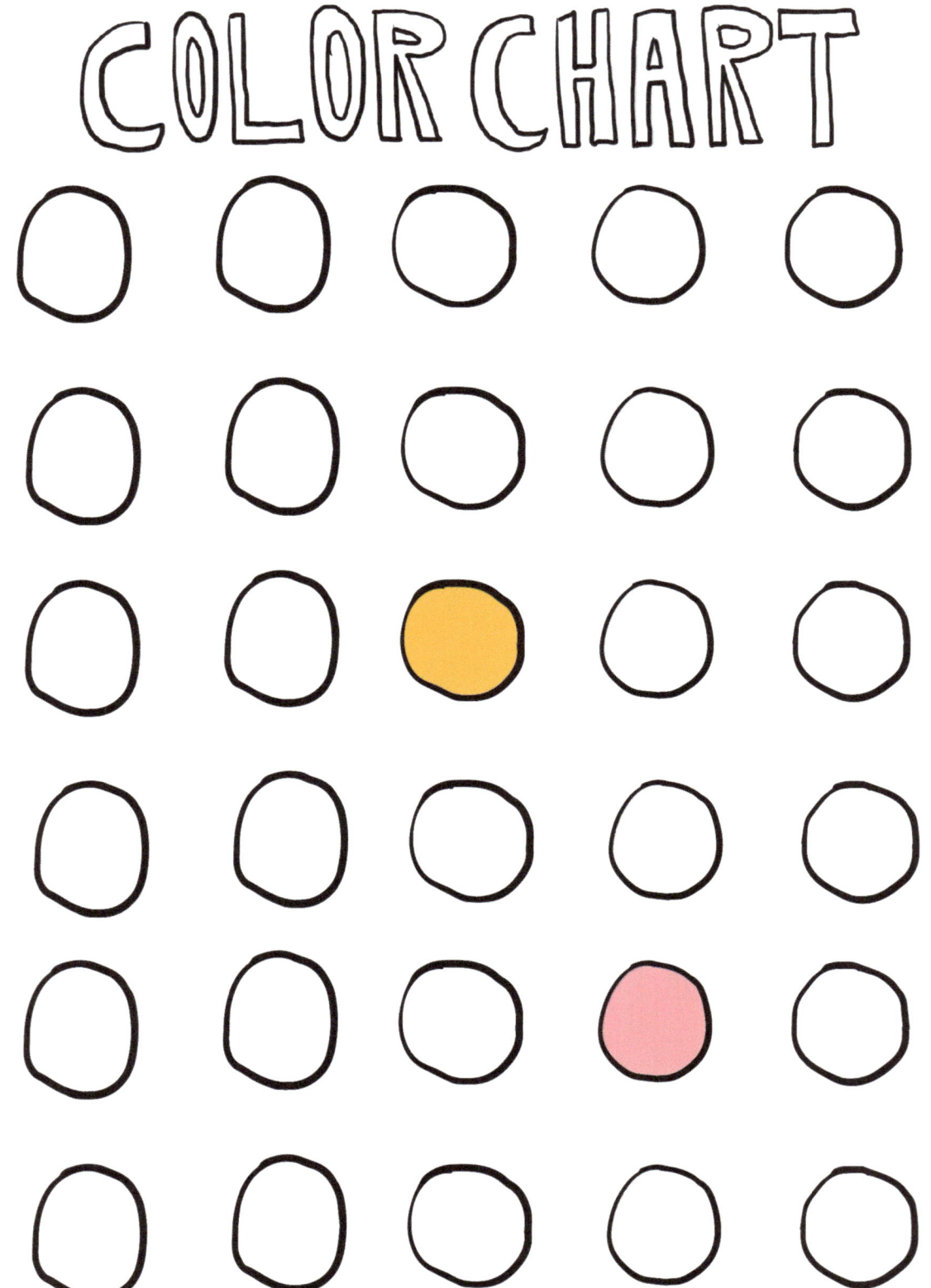

MIX AND MATCH COLORS / LAYER AND EXPERIMENT / TEST

TEXTURE CHART

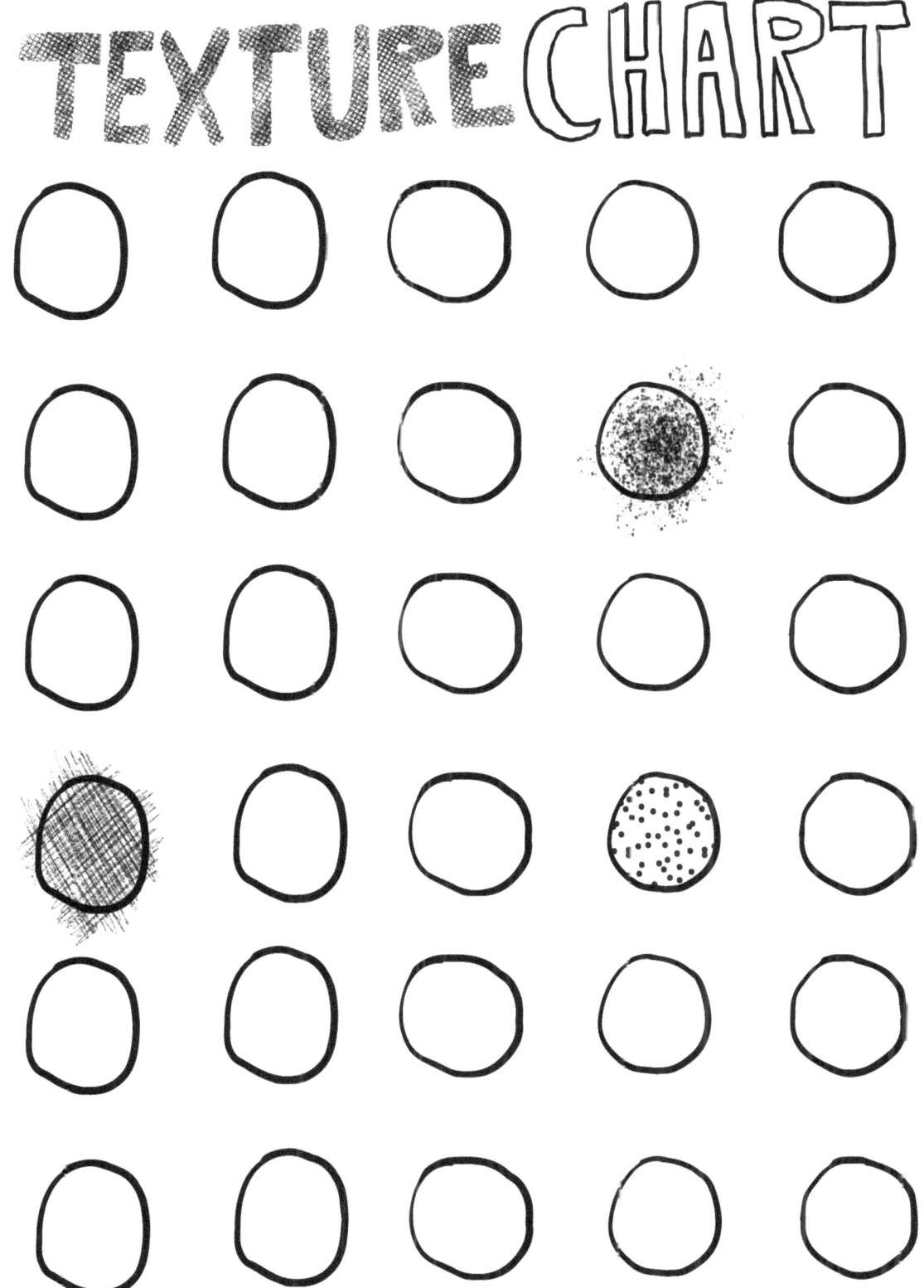

TEST CUT YOUR TEXTURES

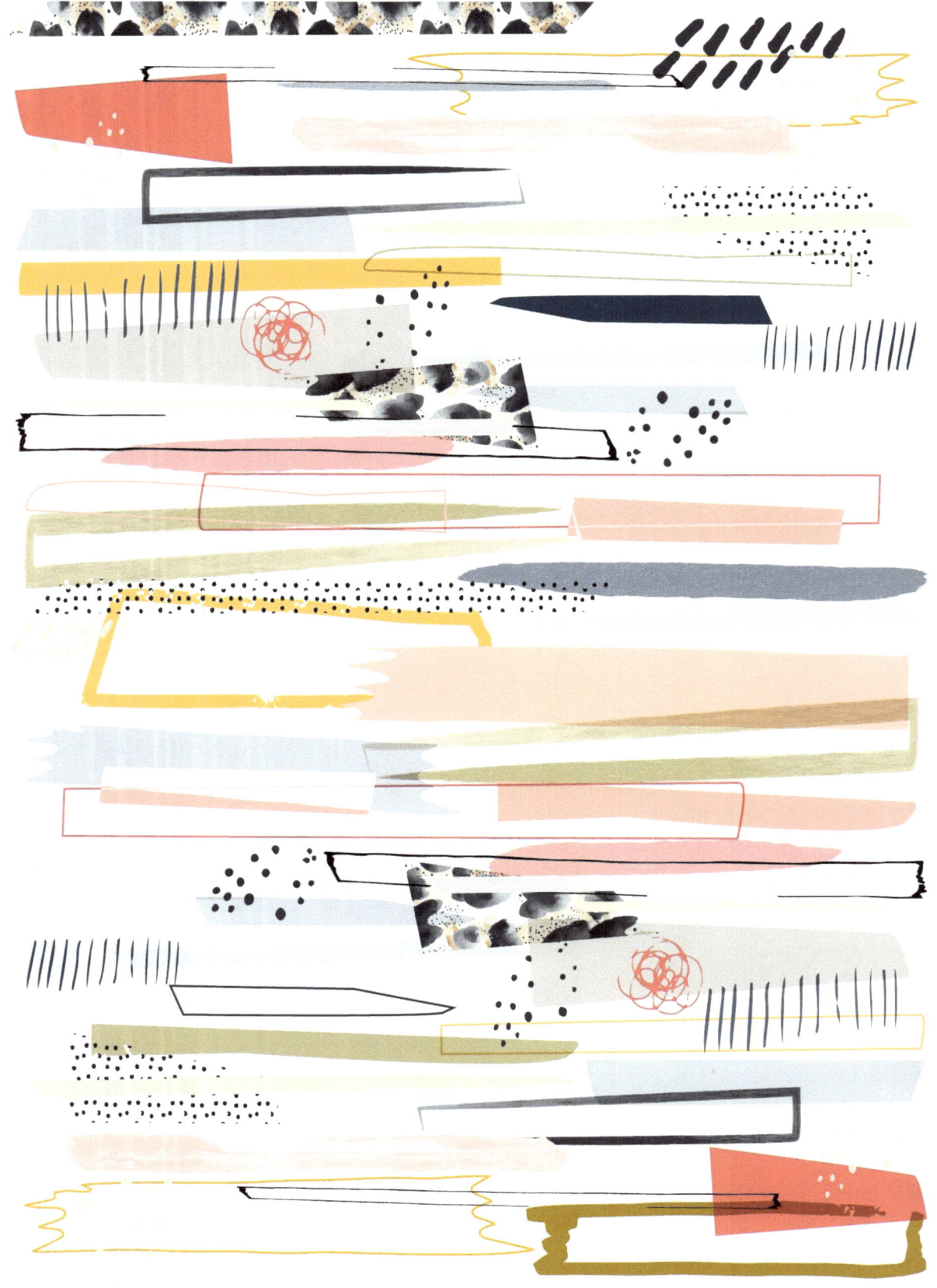

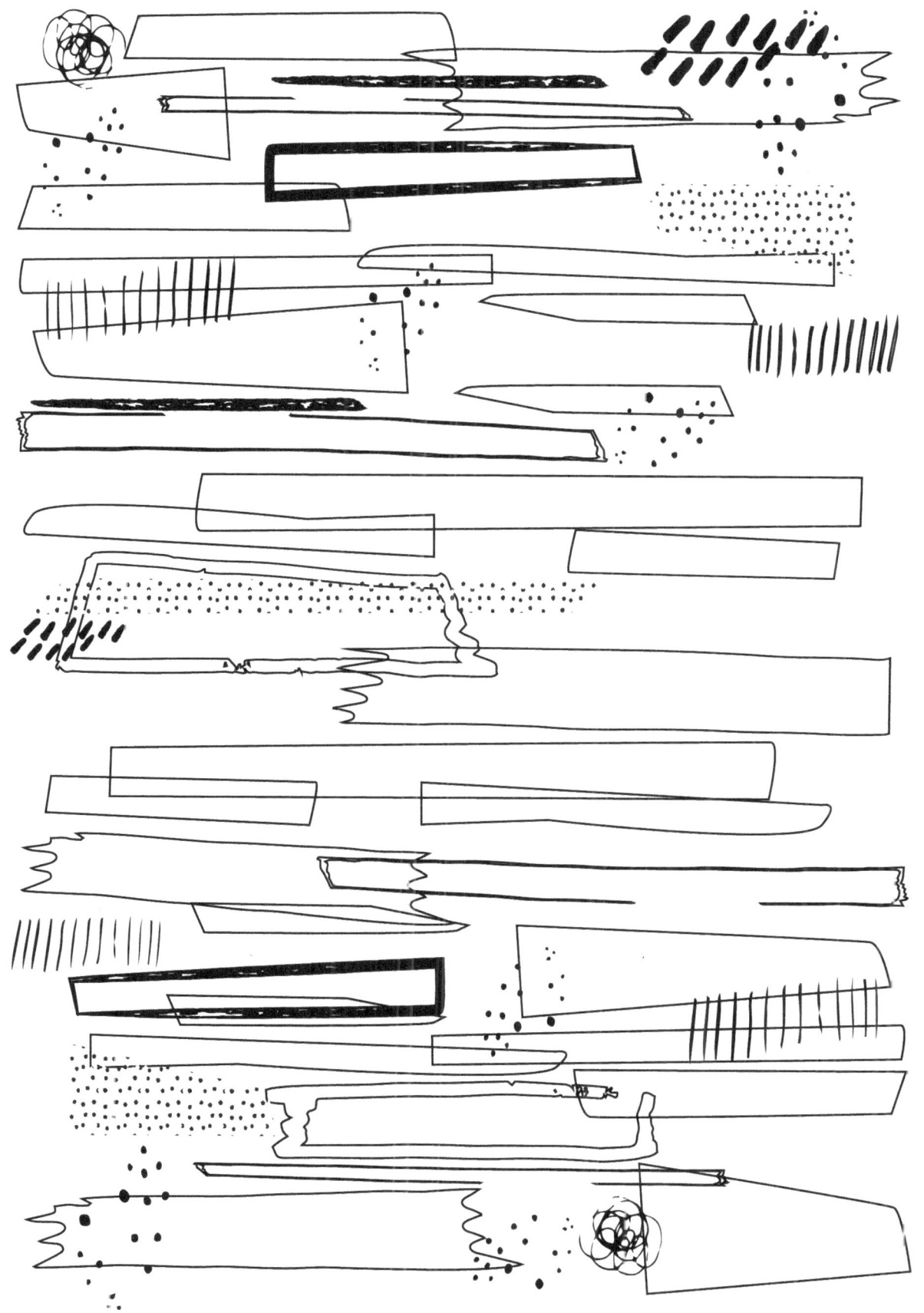

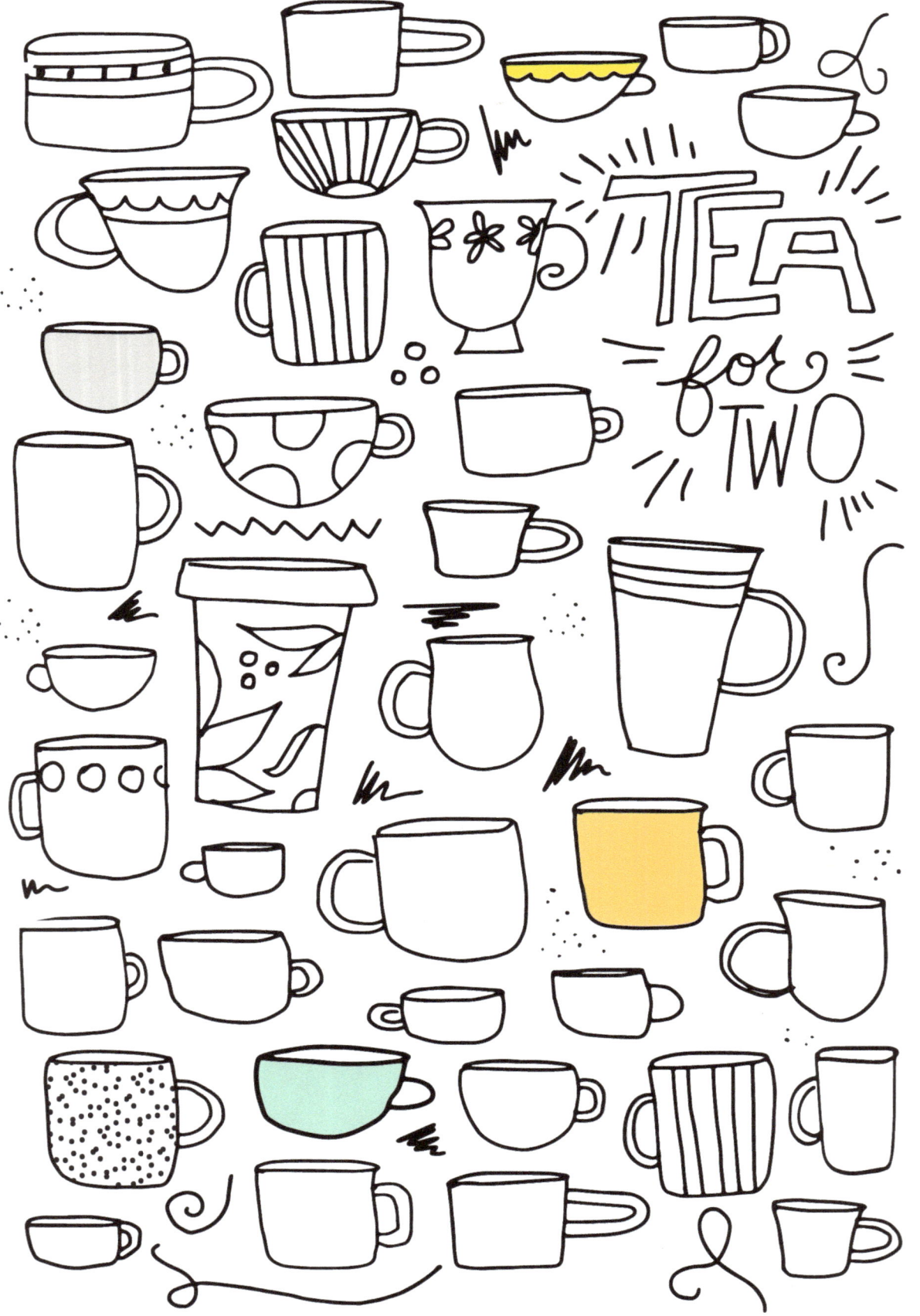

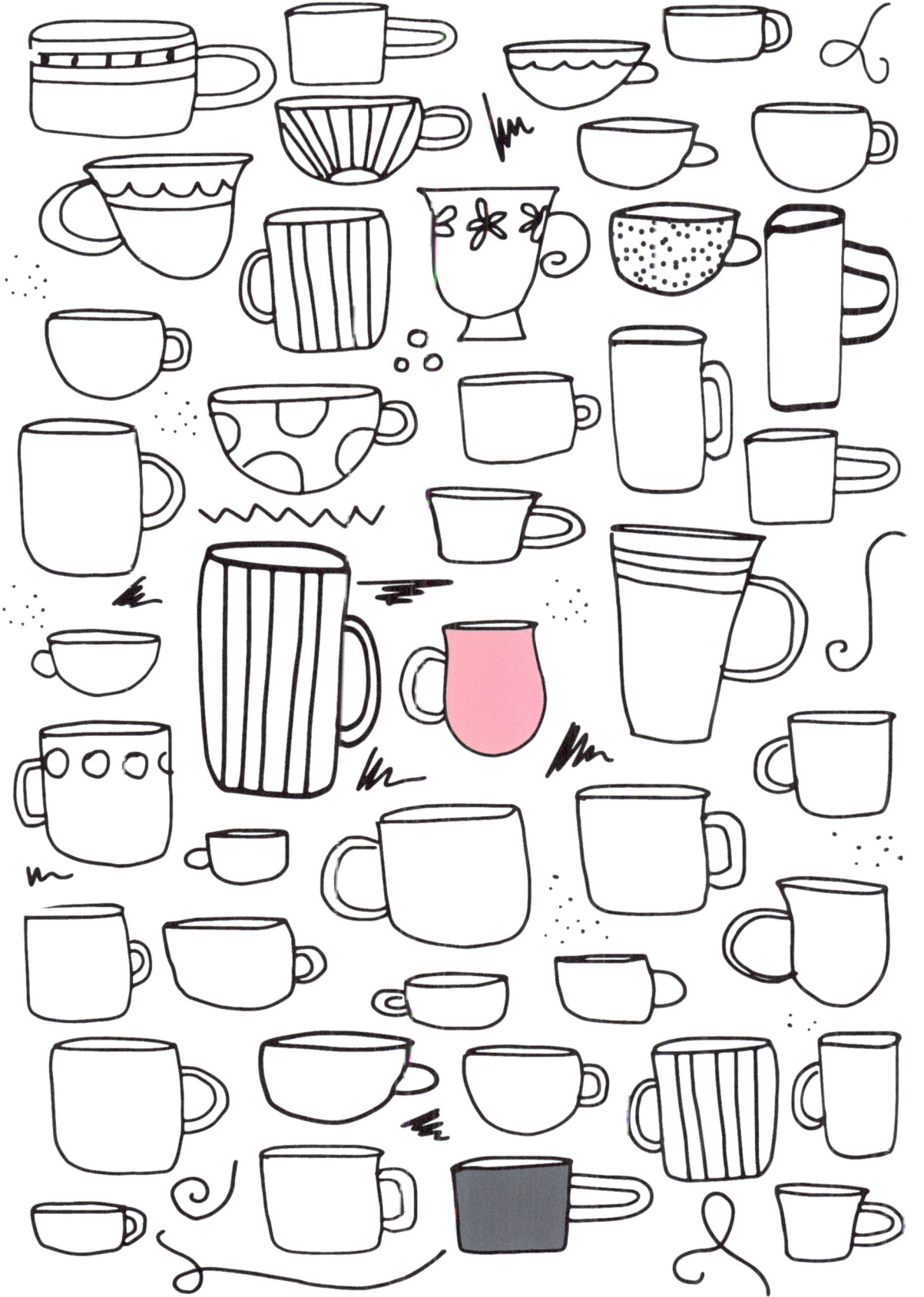

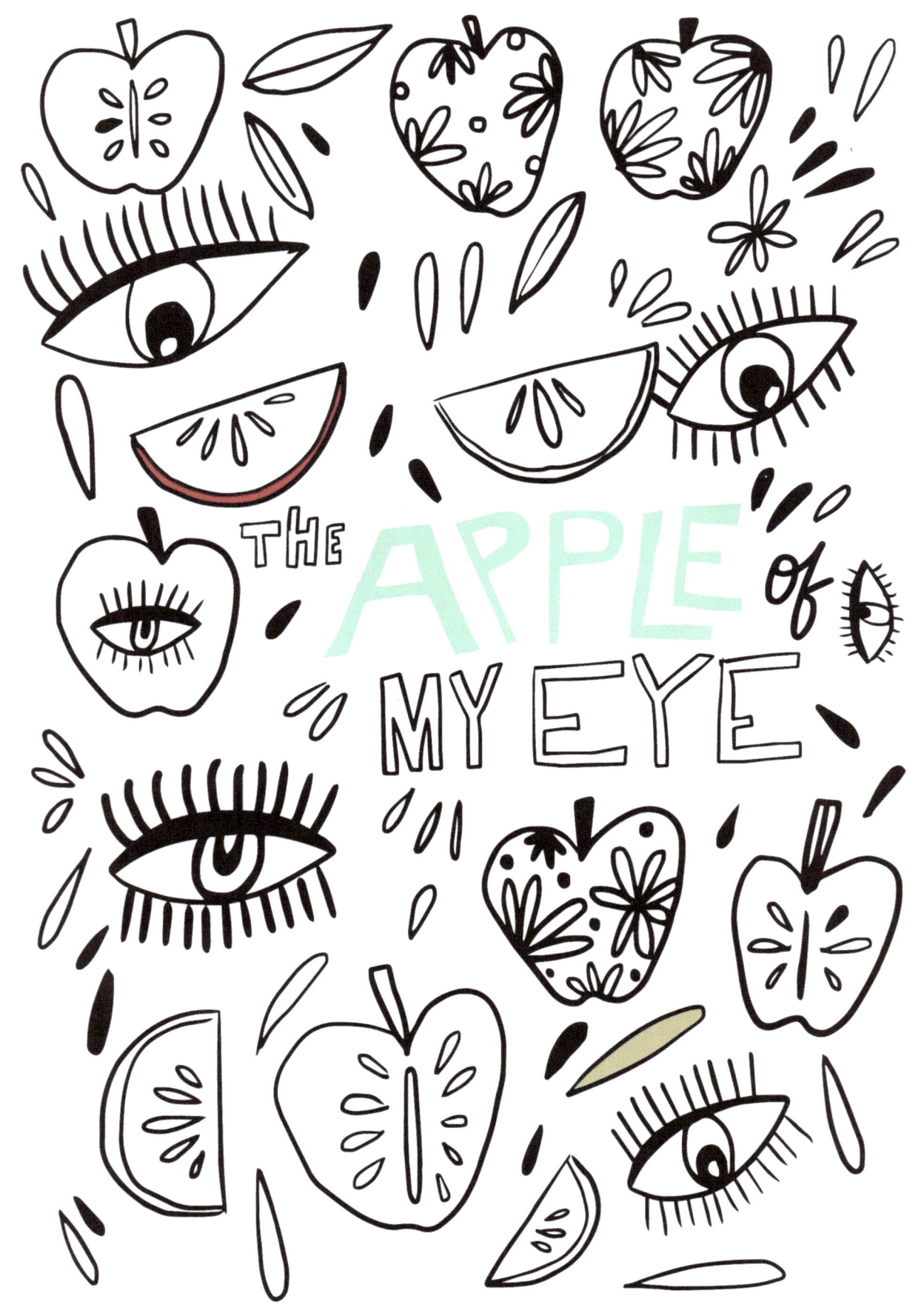

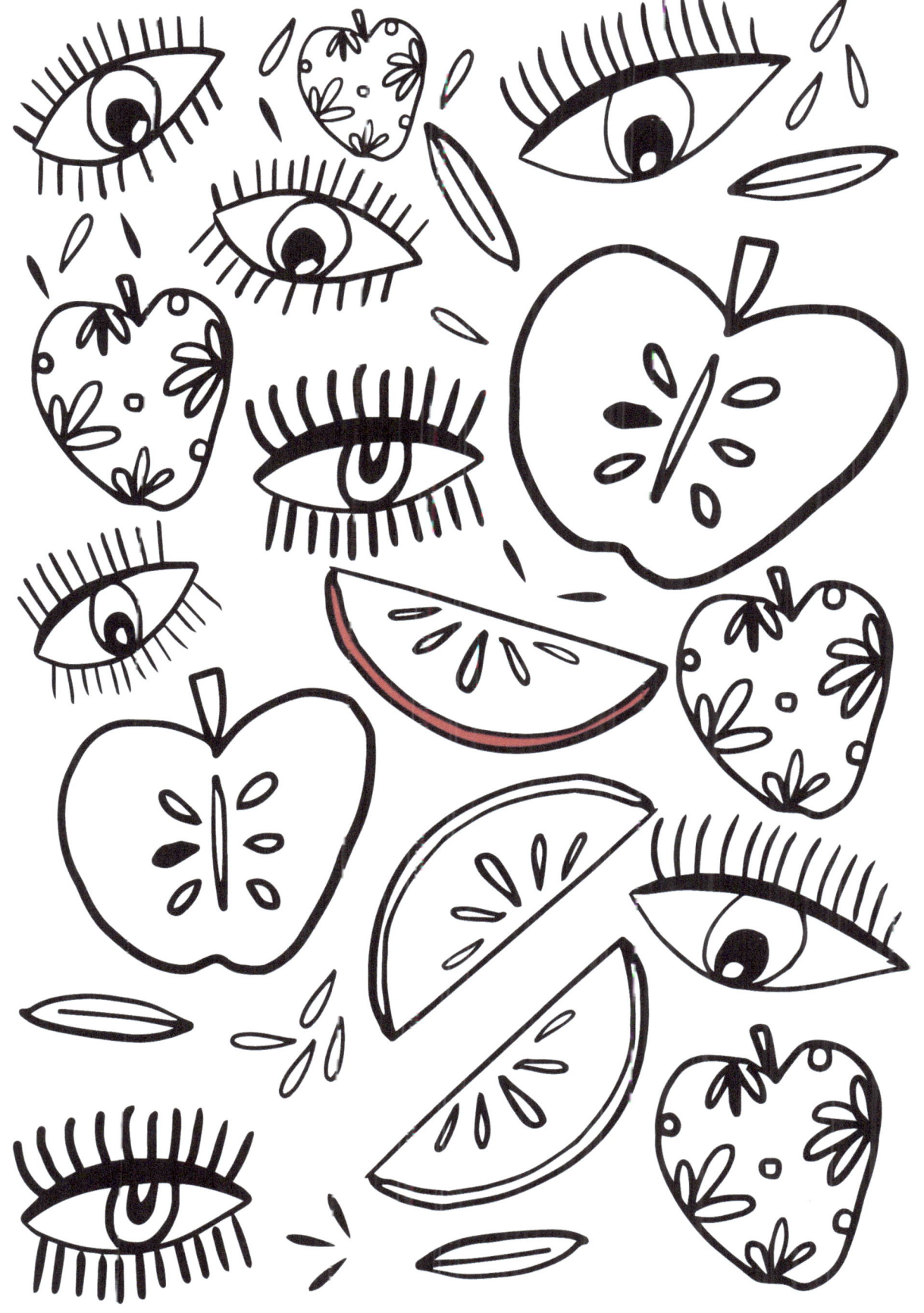

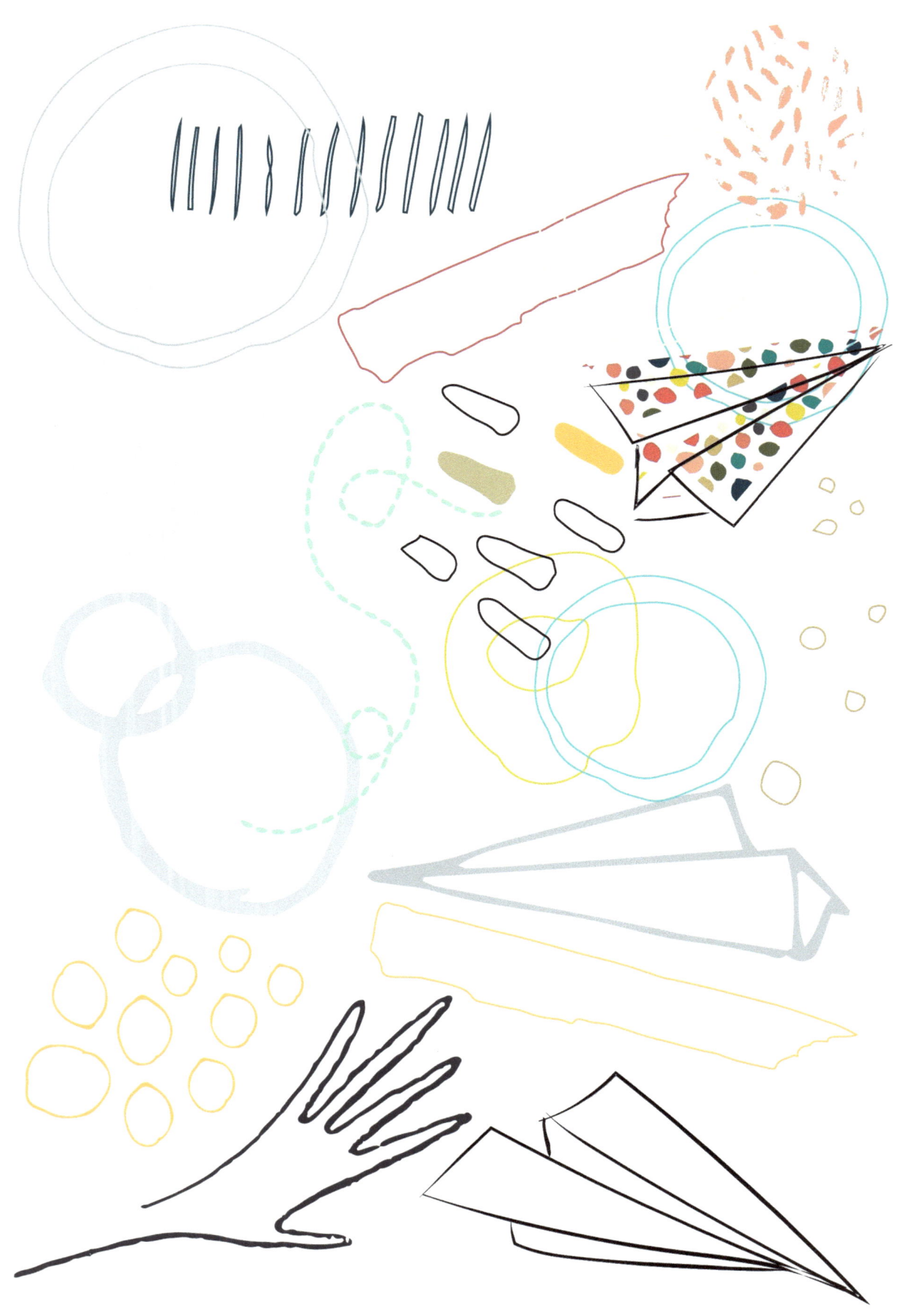

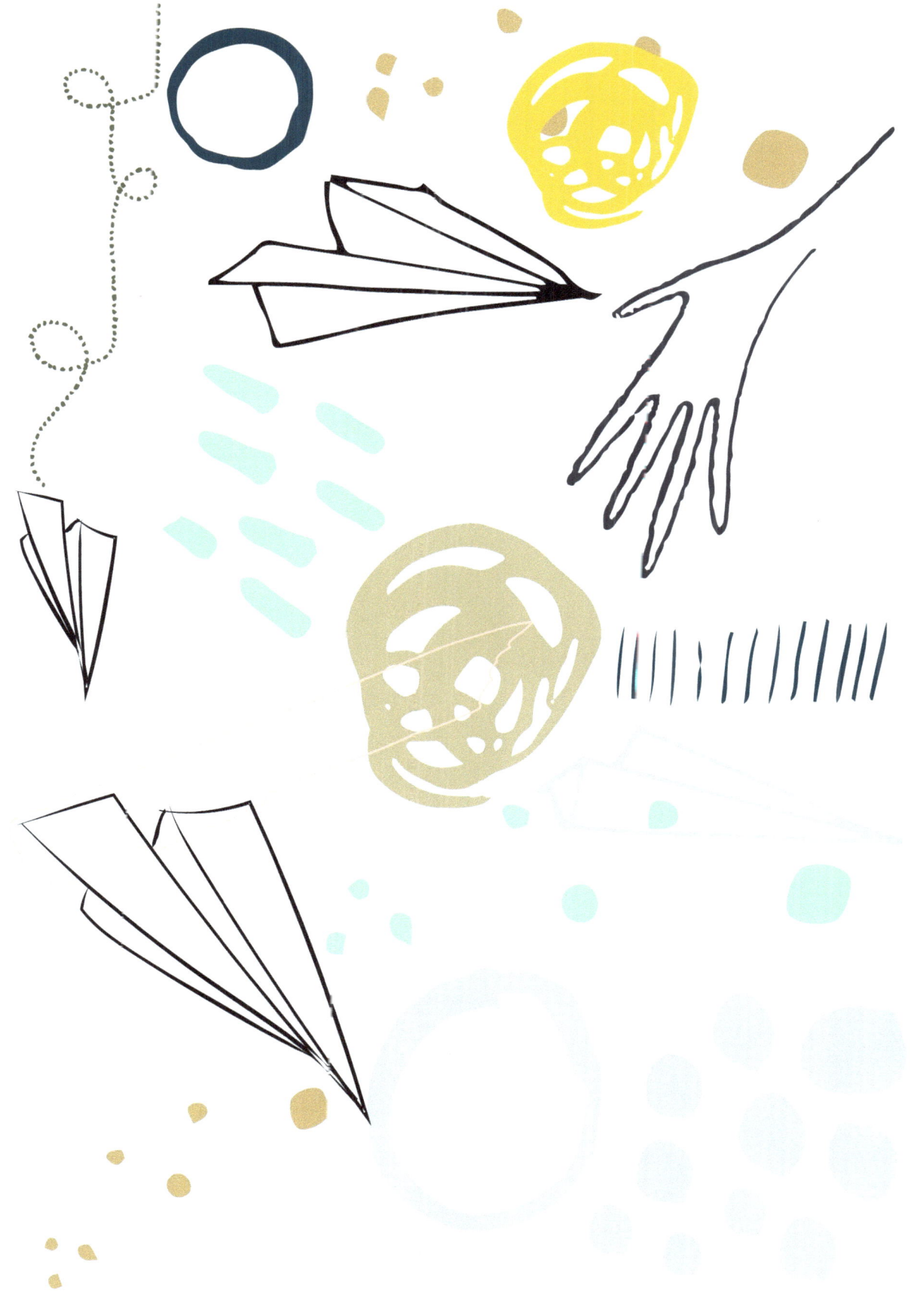

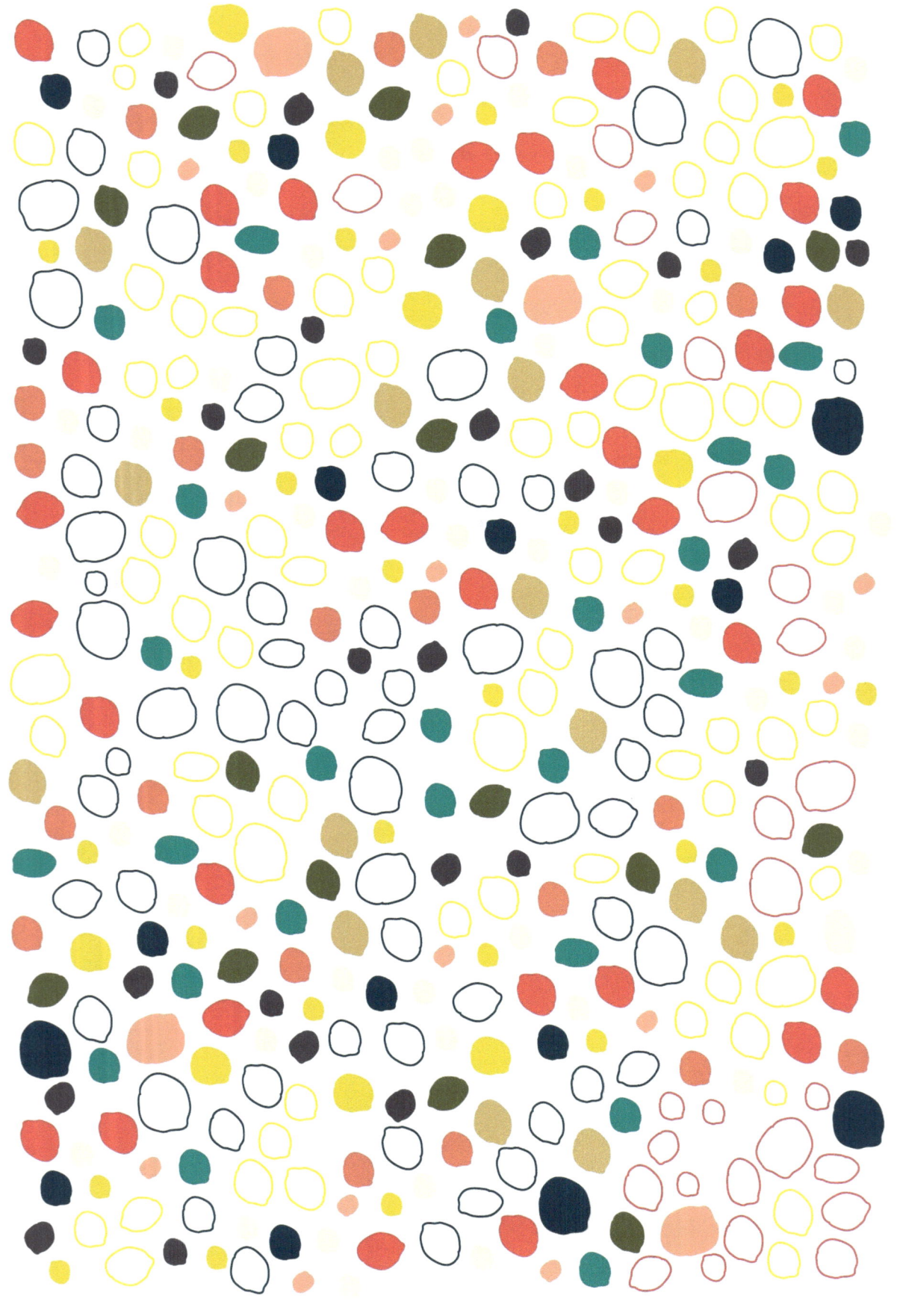

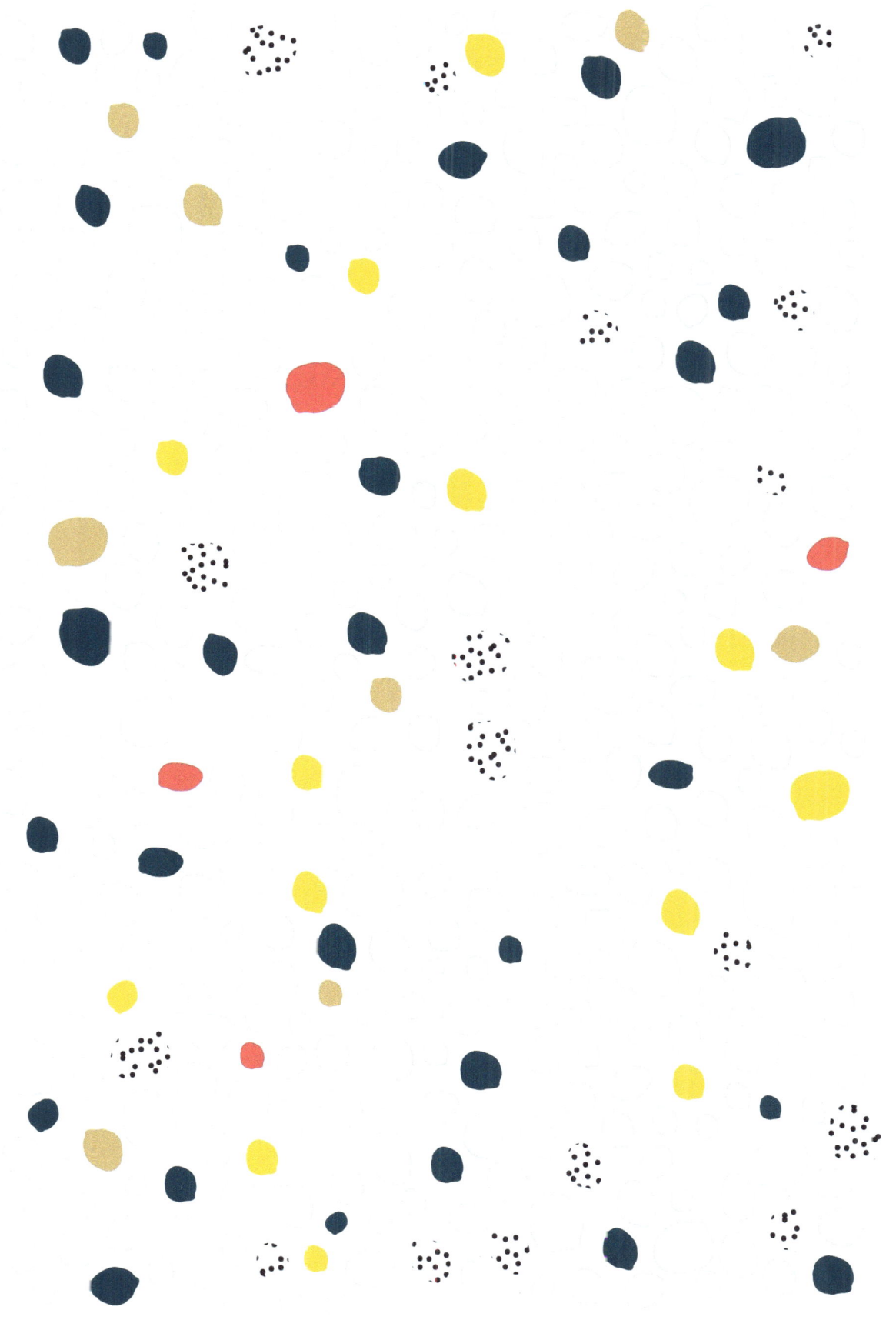

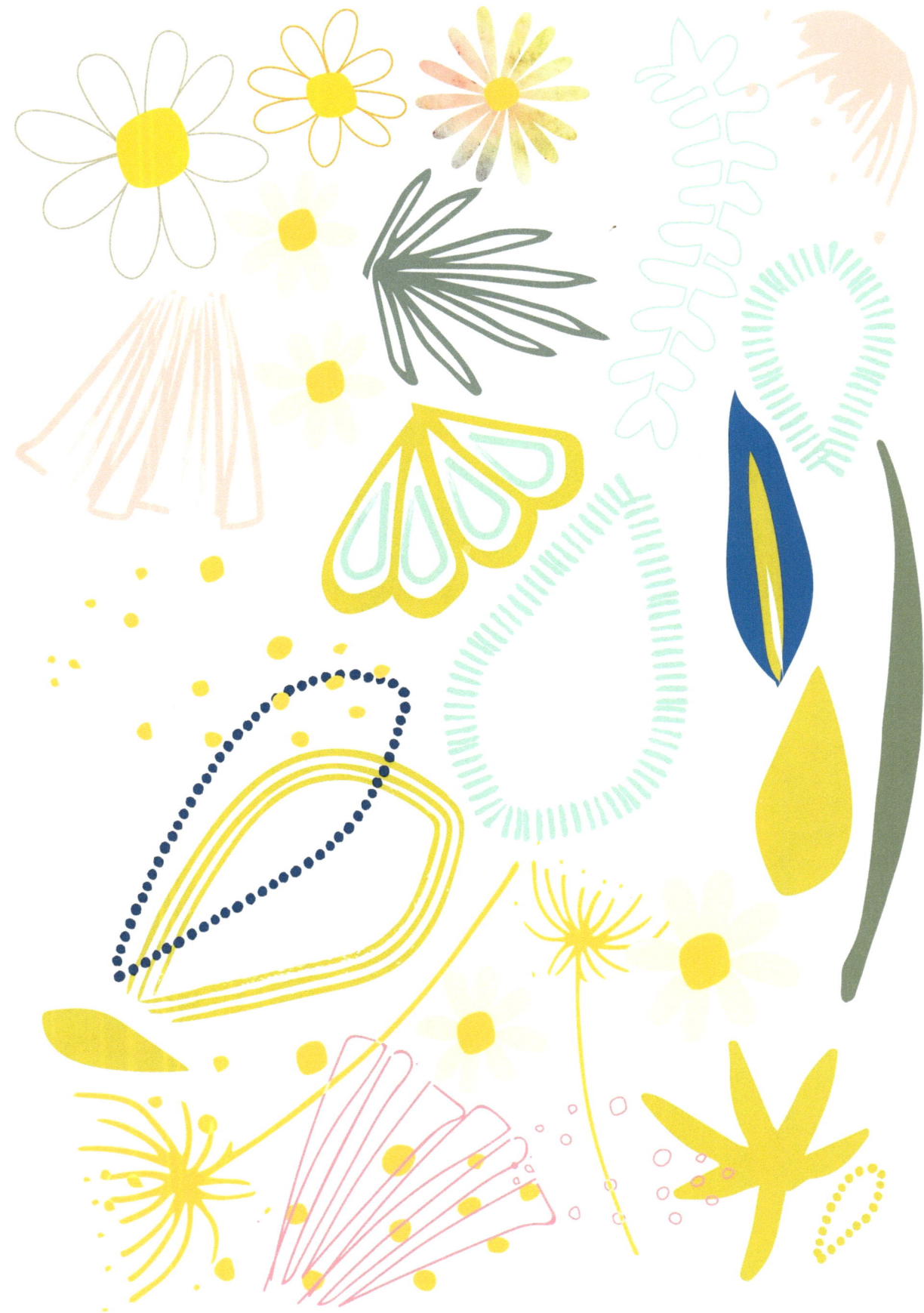

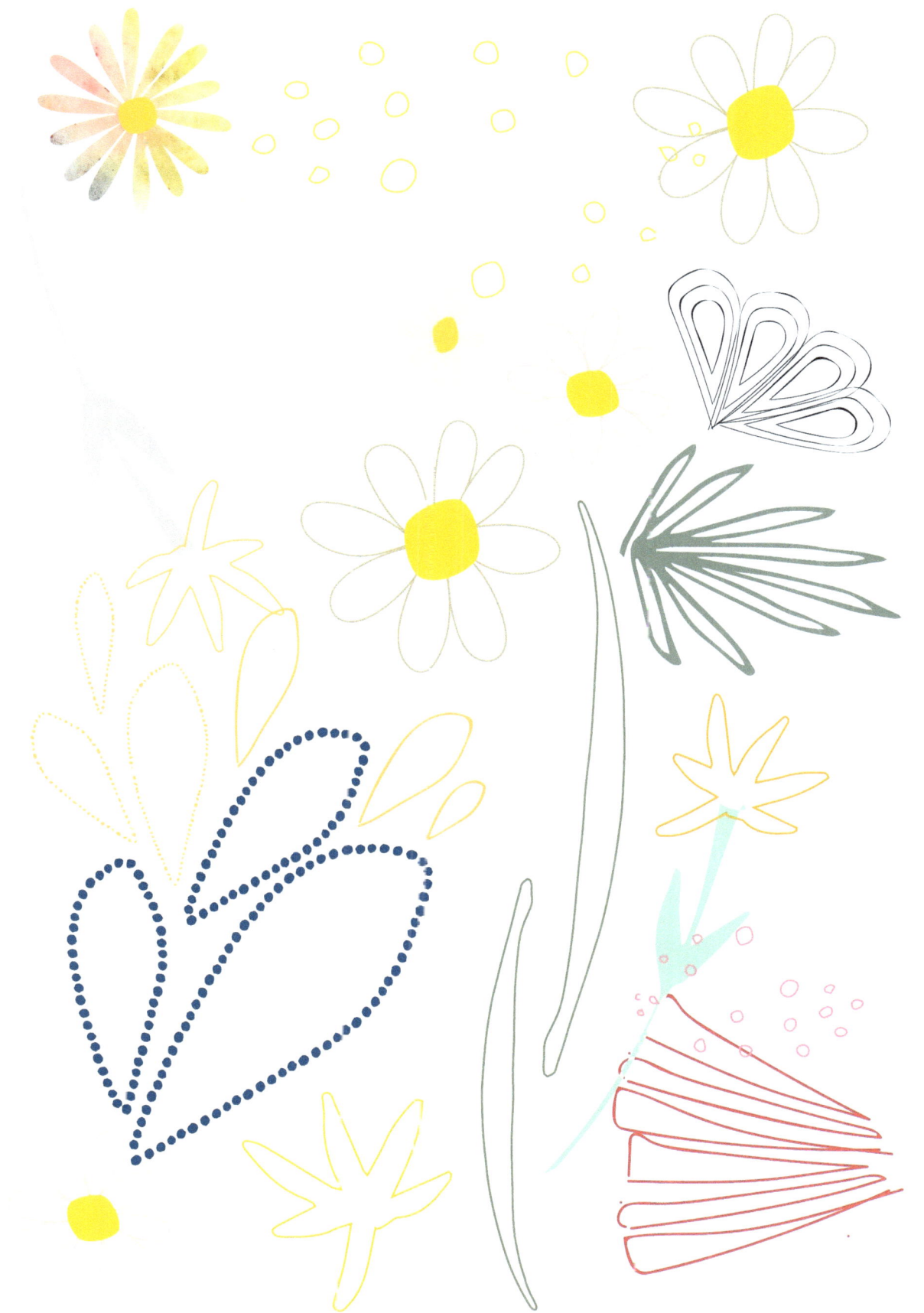

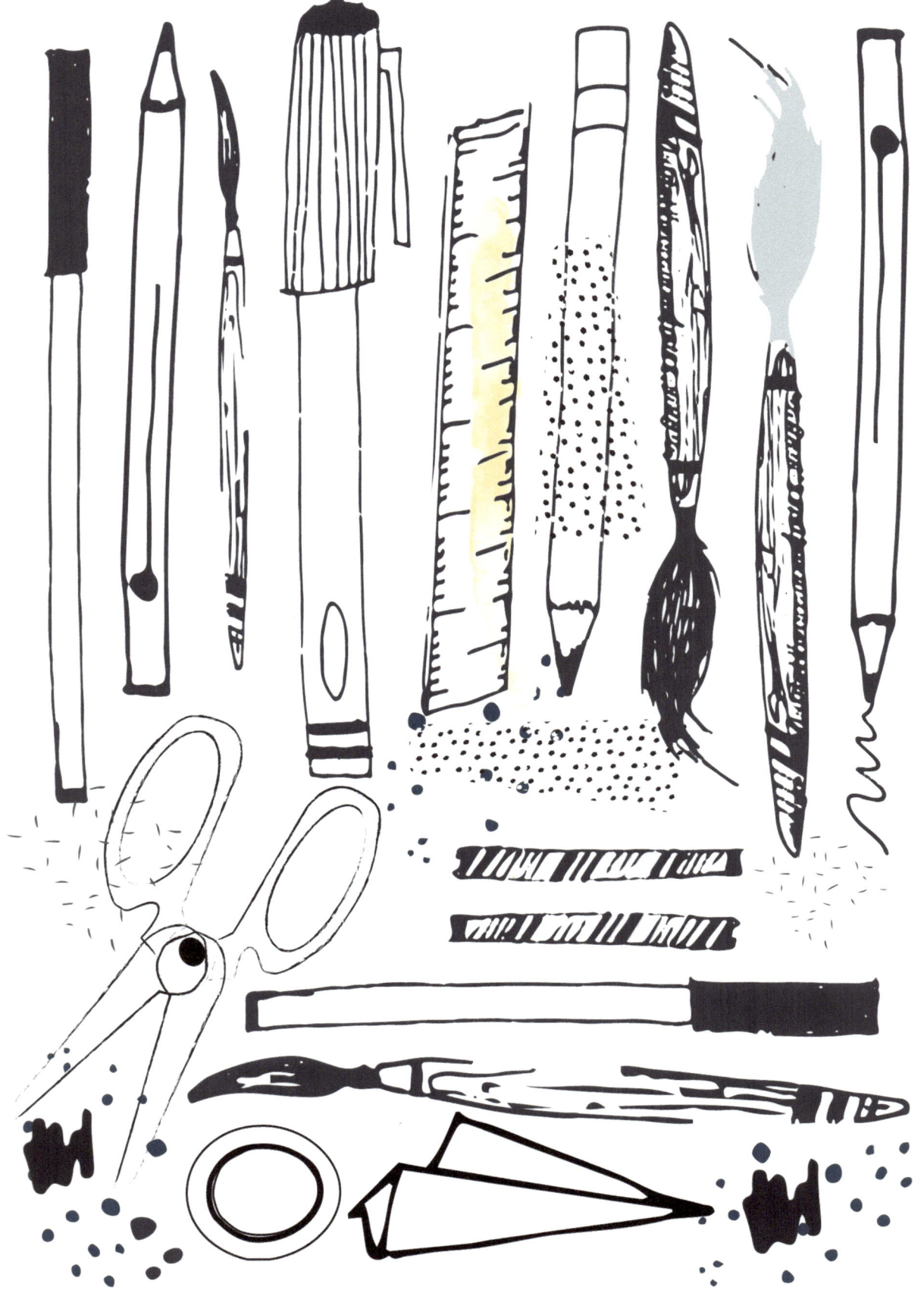

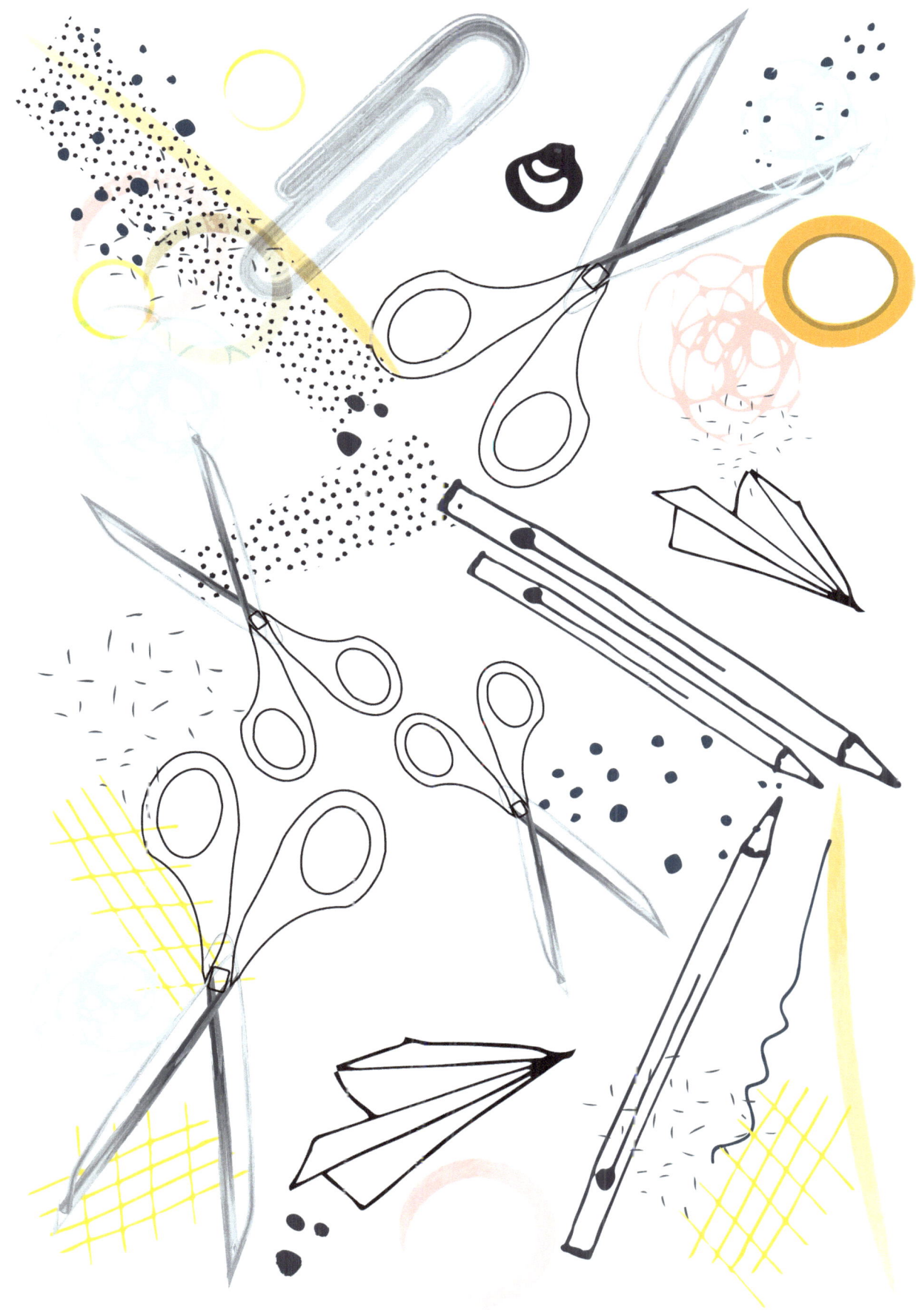

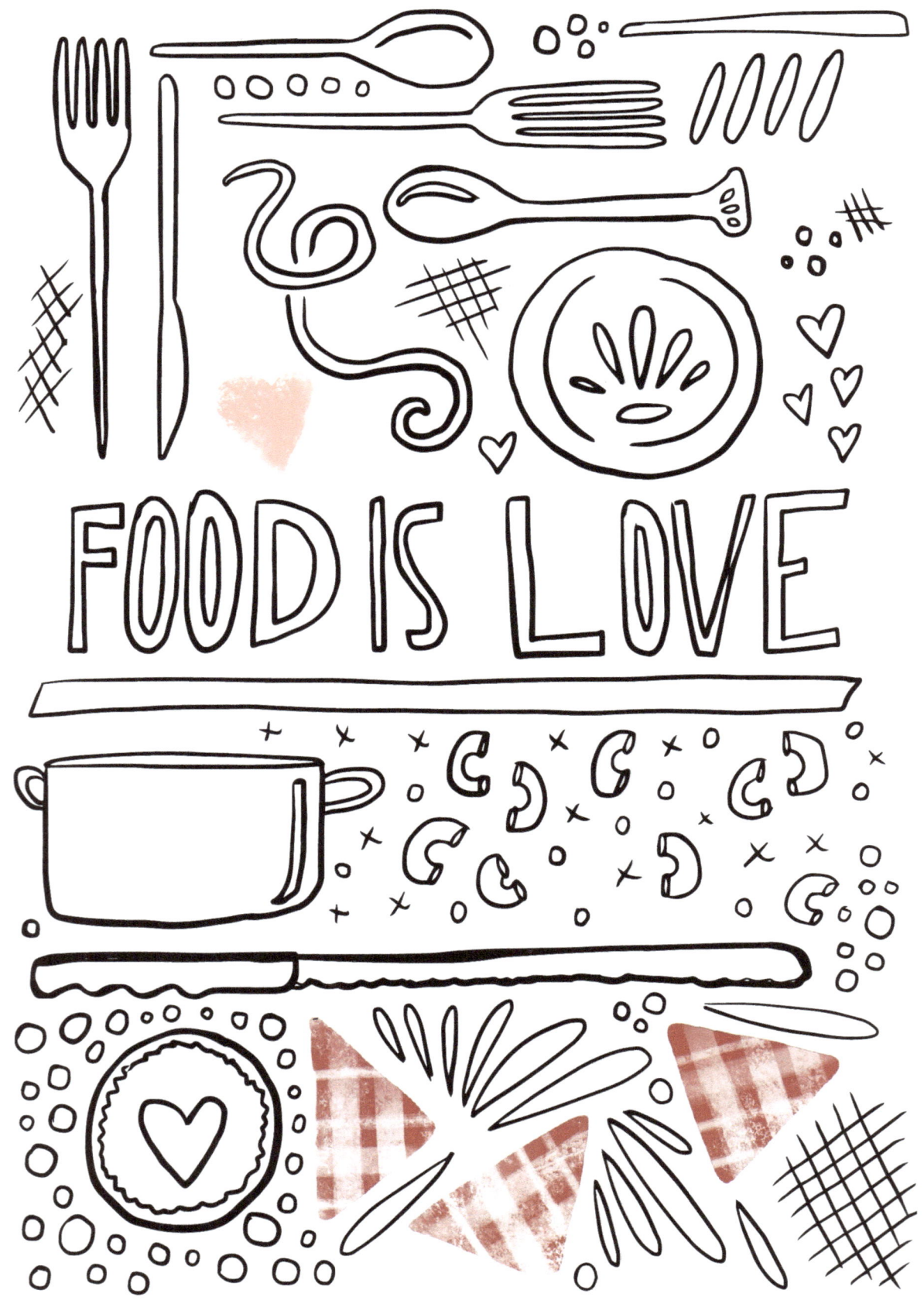

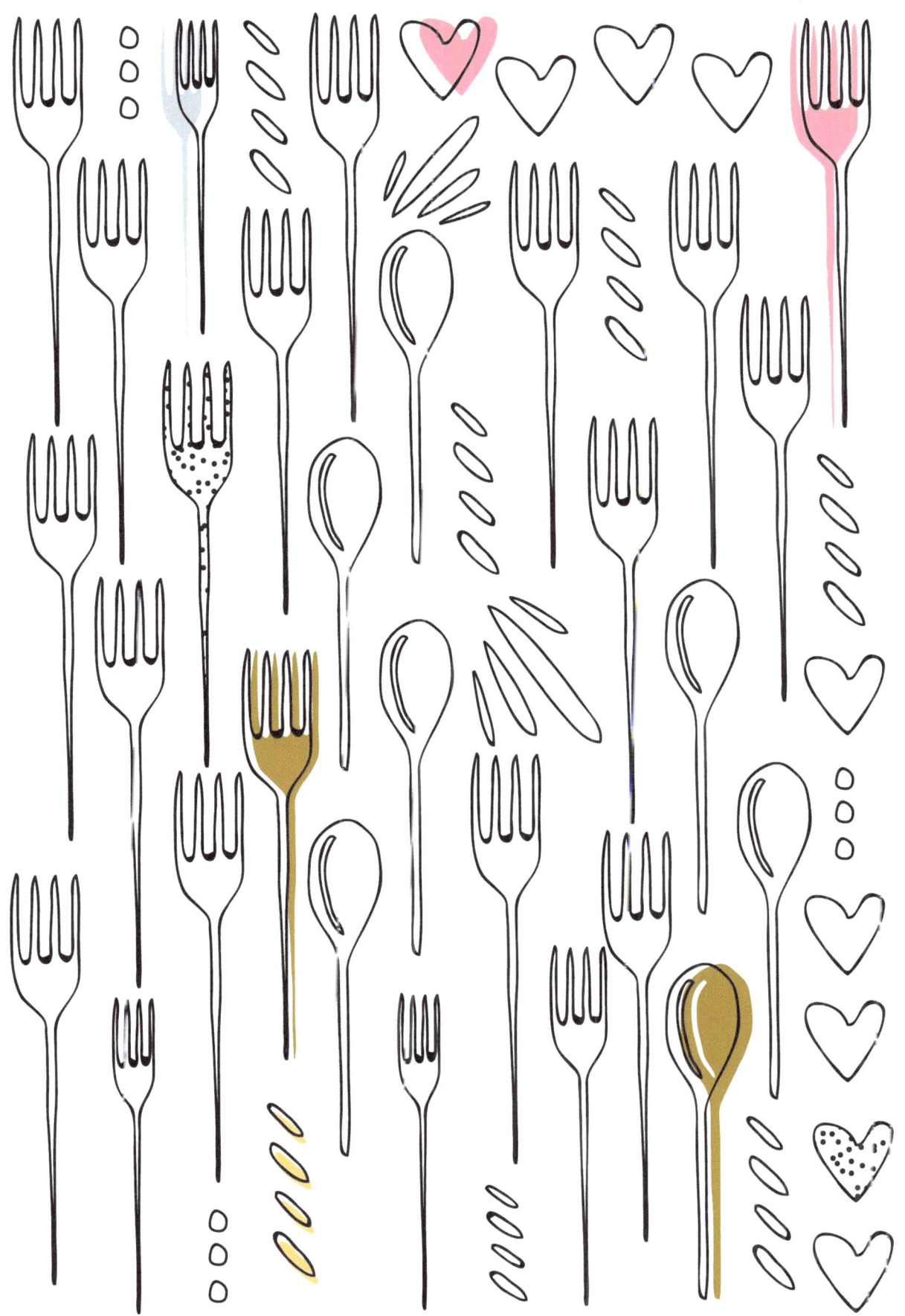

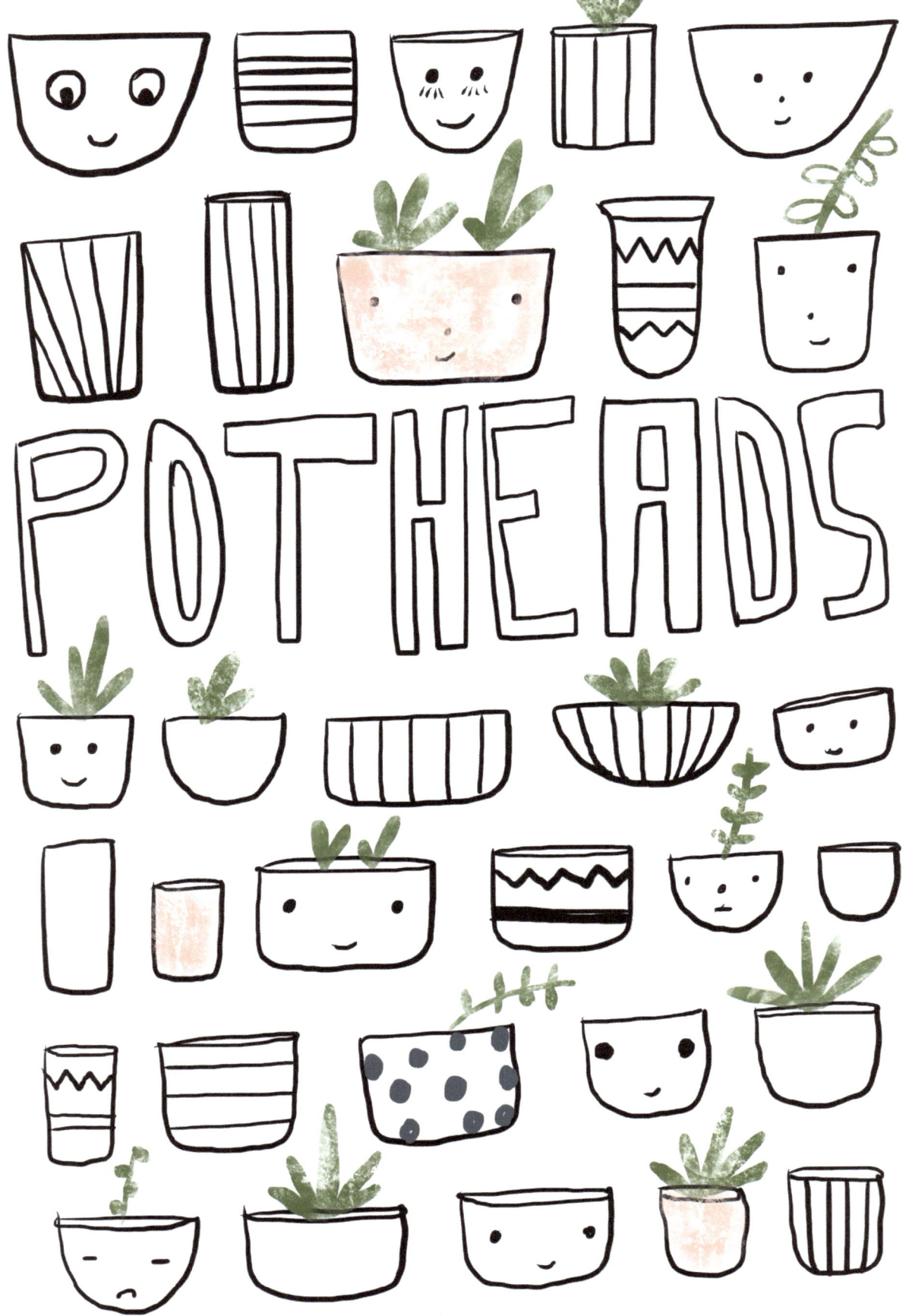

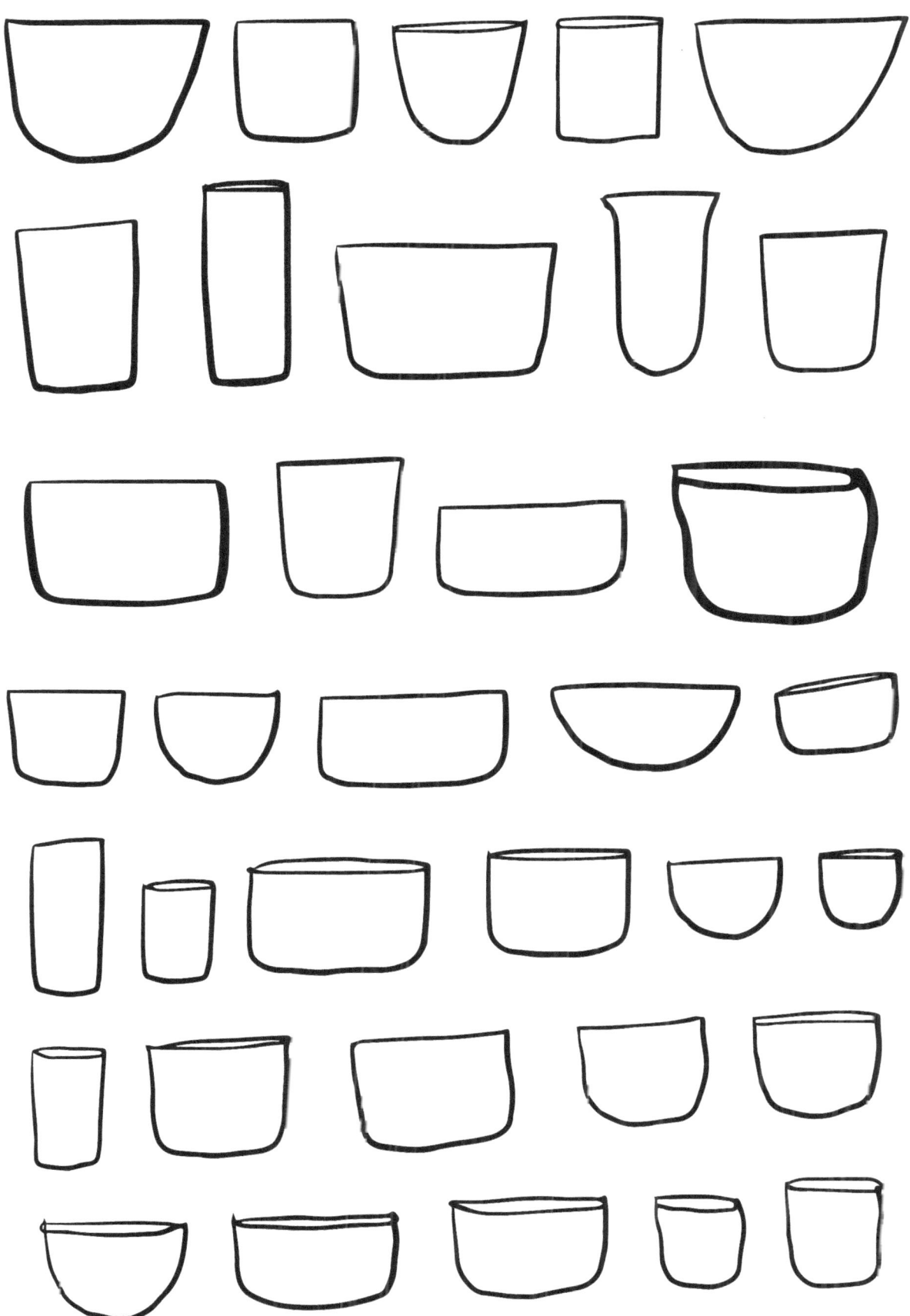

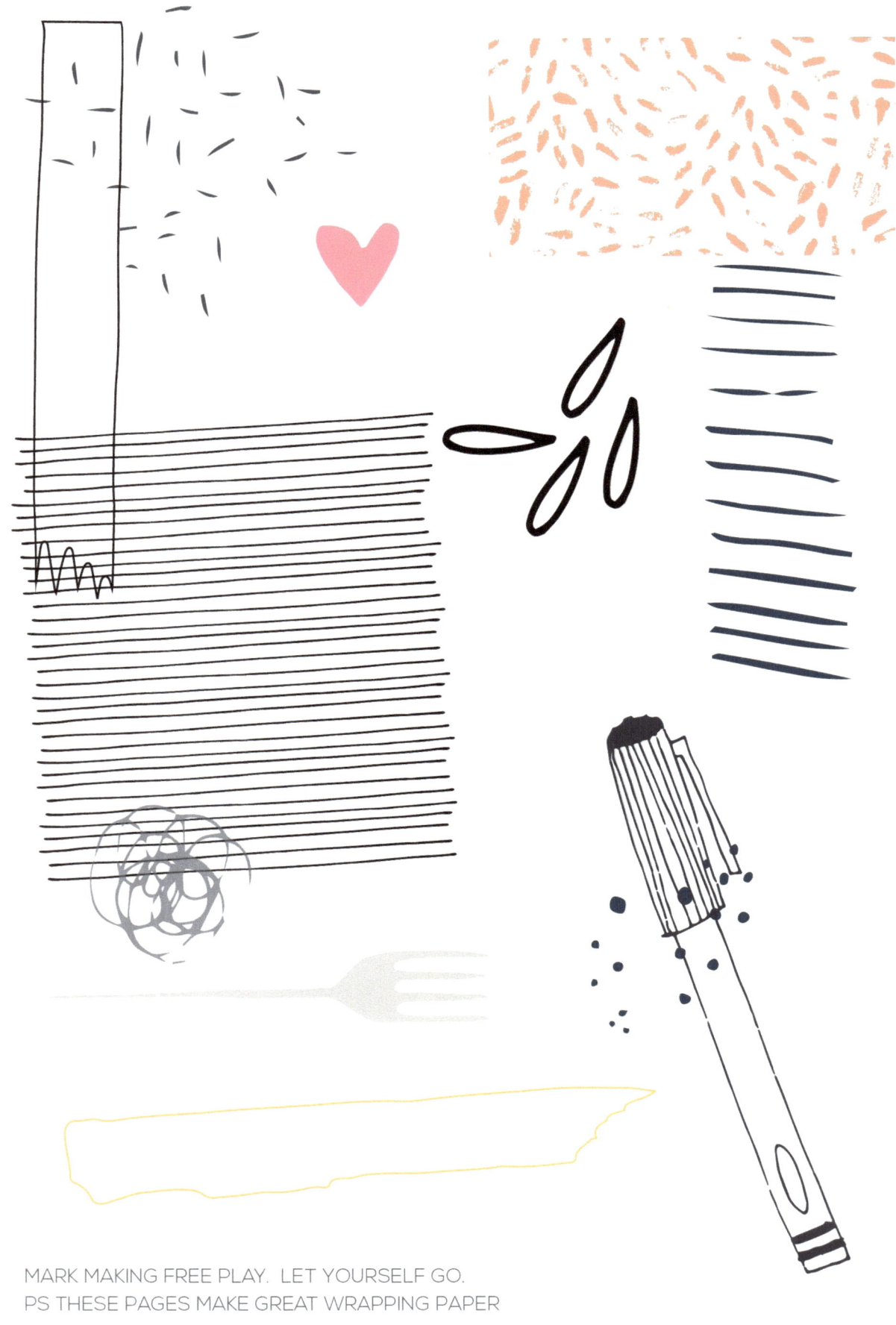

MARK MAKING FREE PLAY. LET YOURSELF GO.
PS THESE PAGES MAKE GREAT WRAPPING PAPER

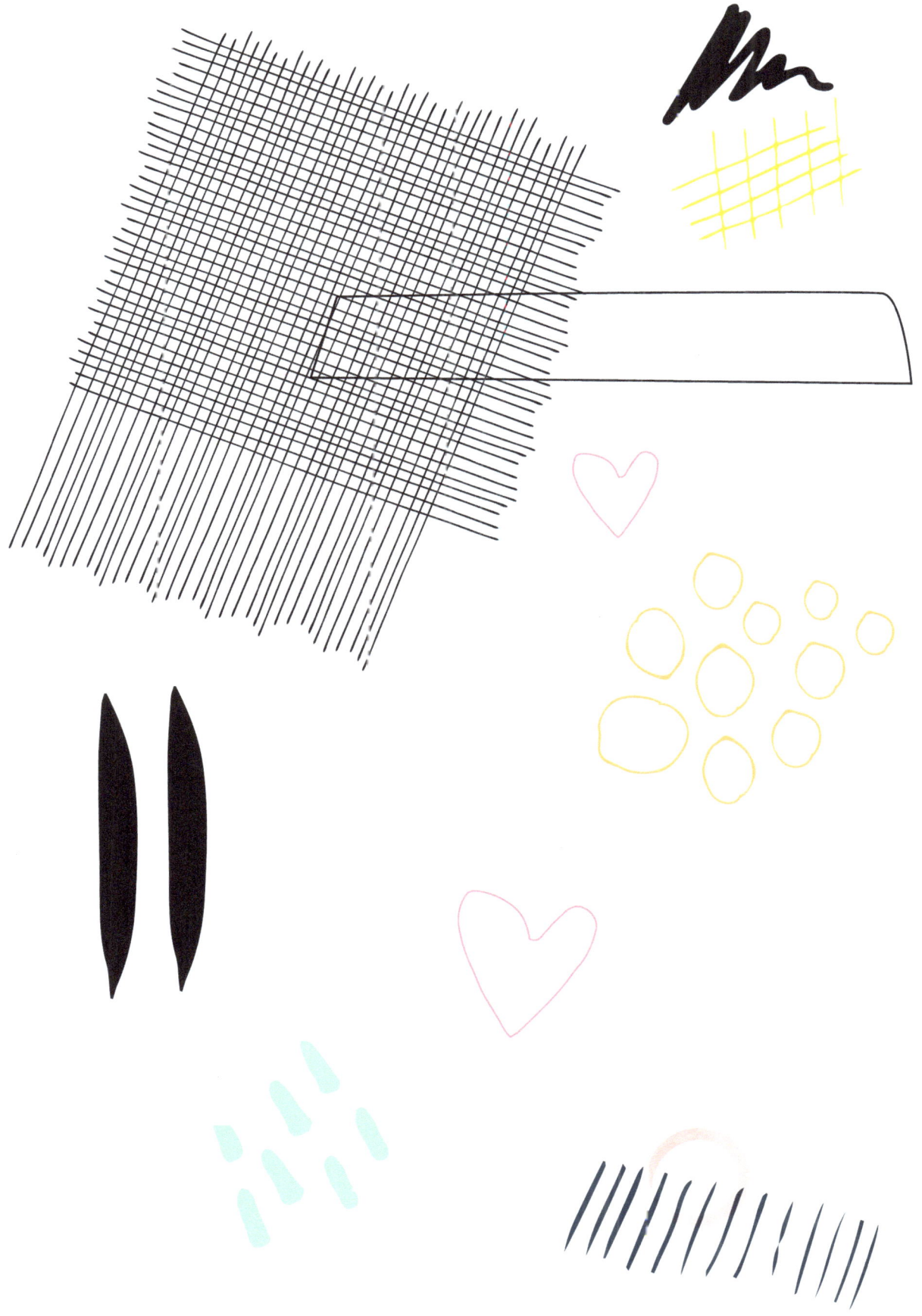

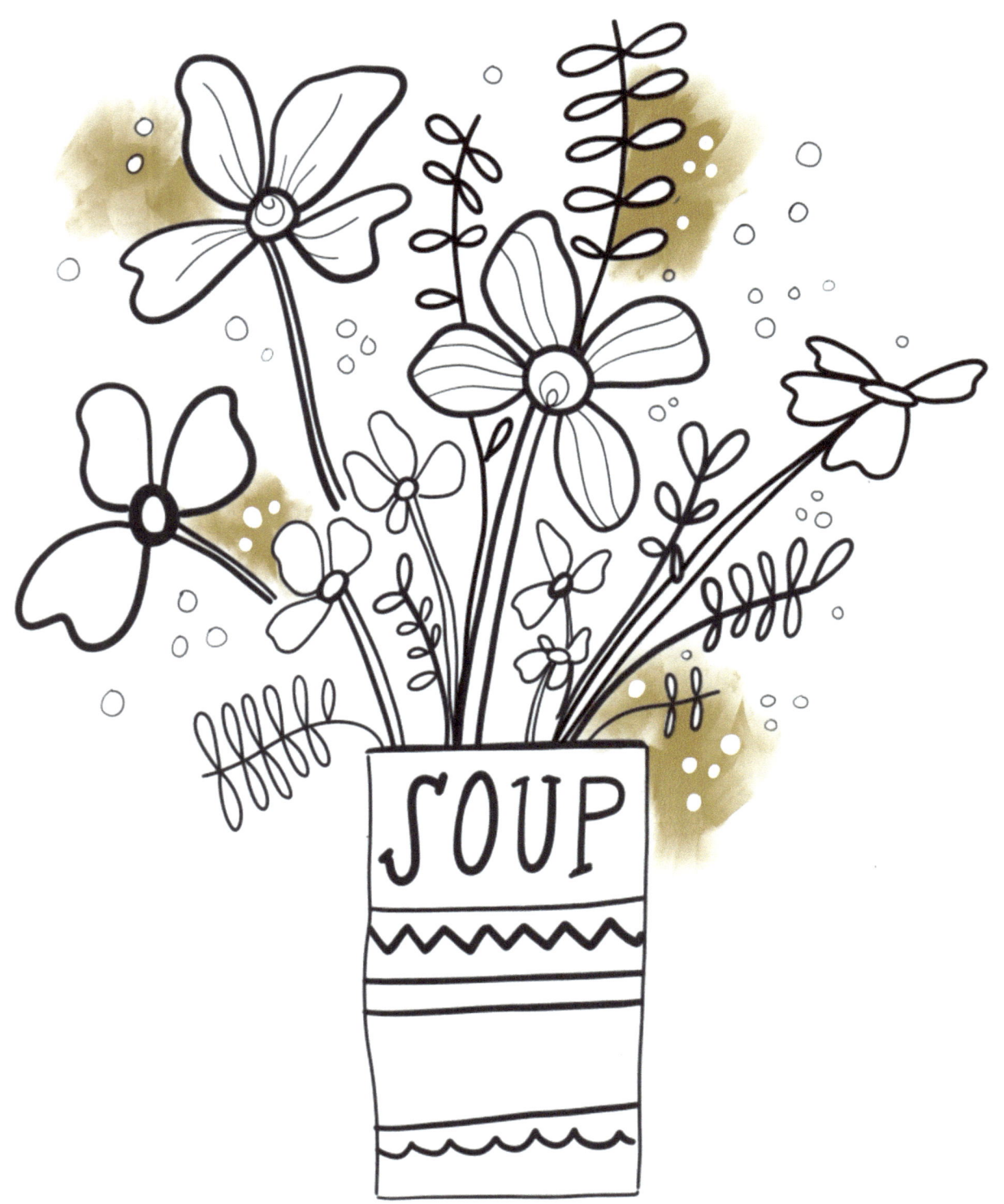

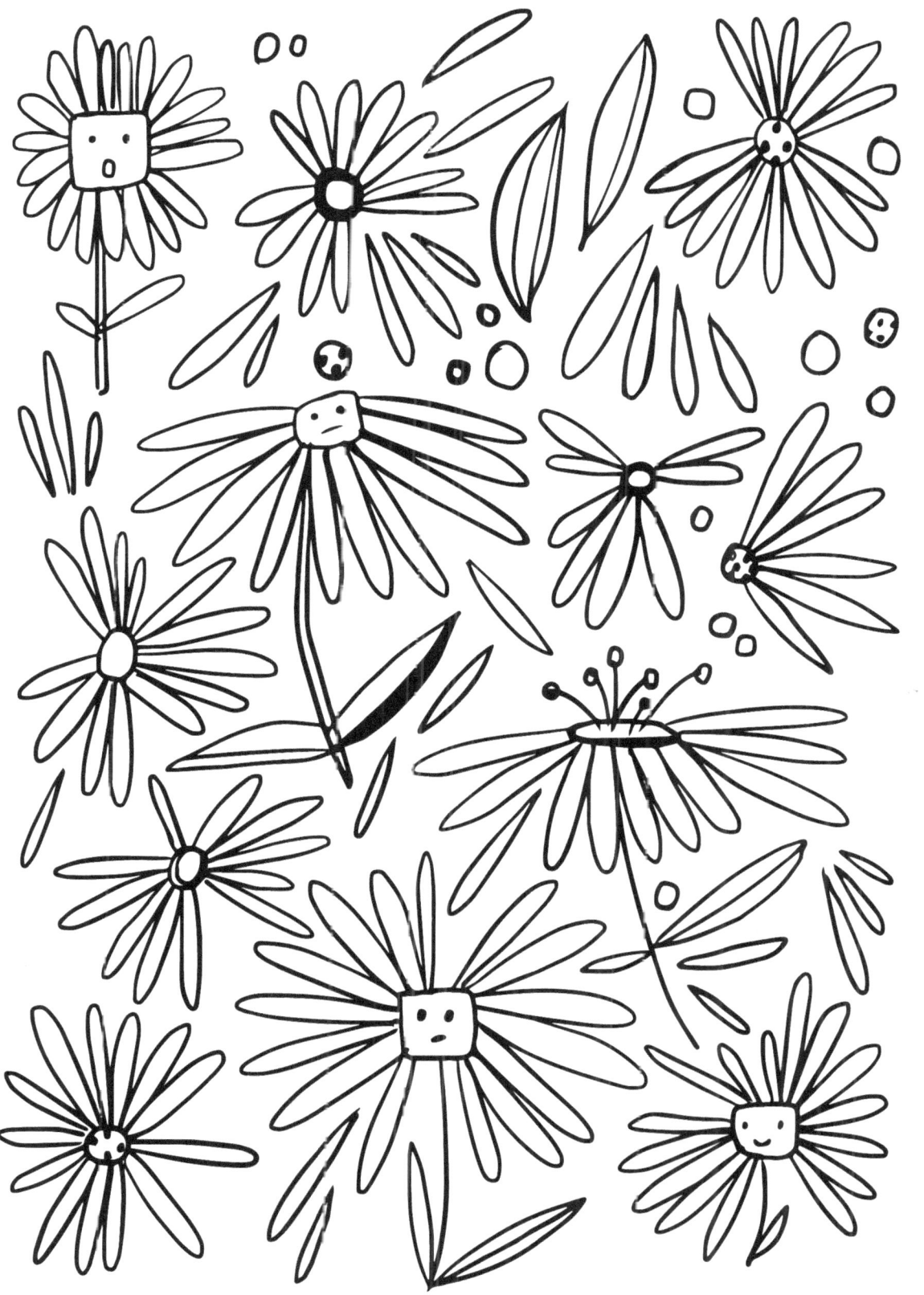

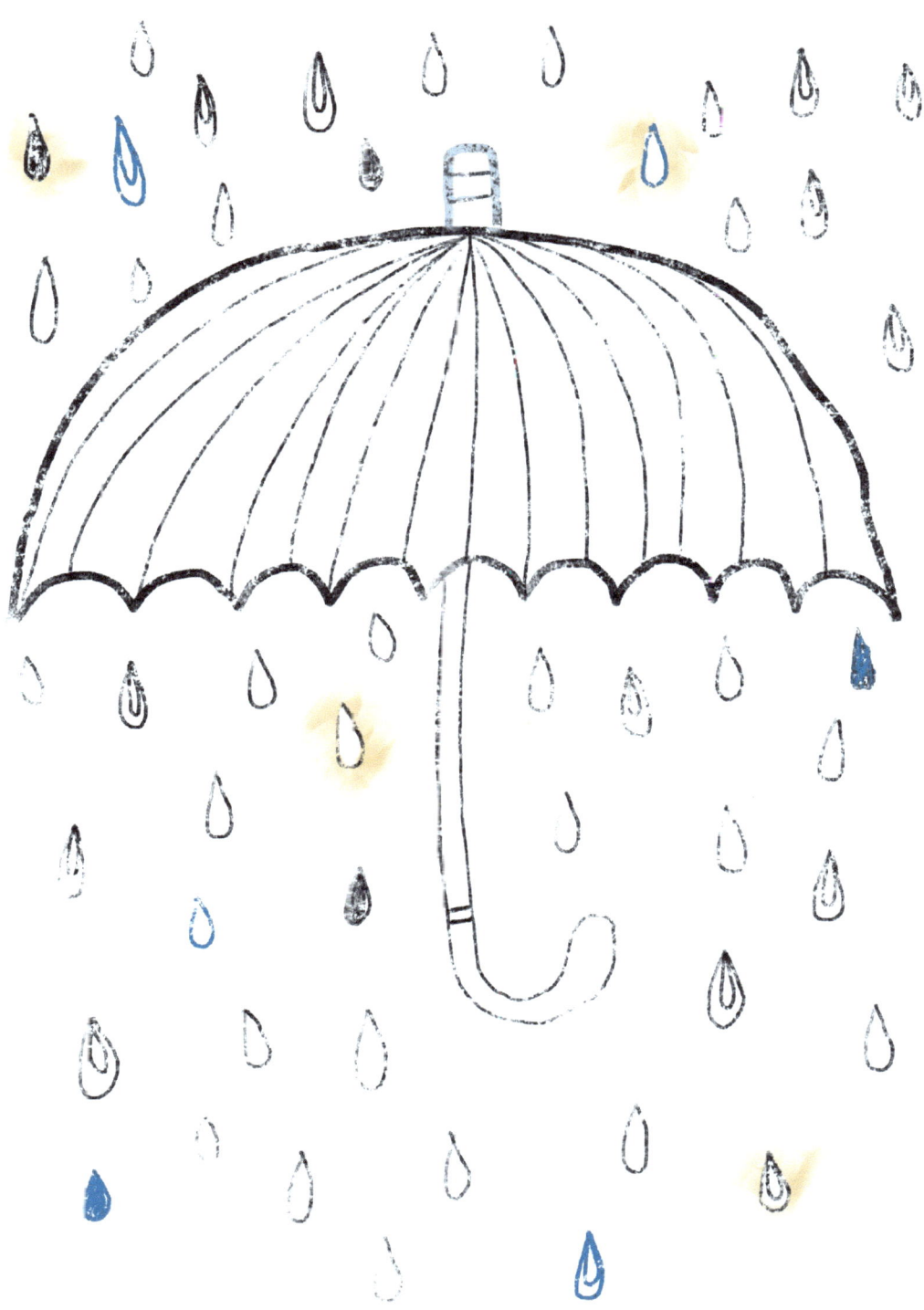

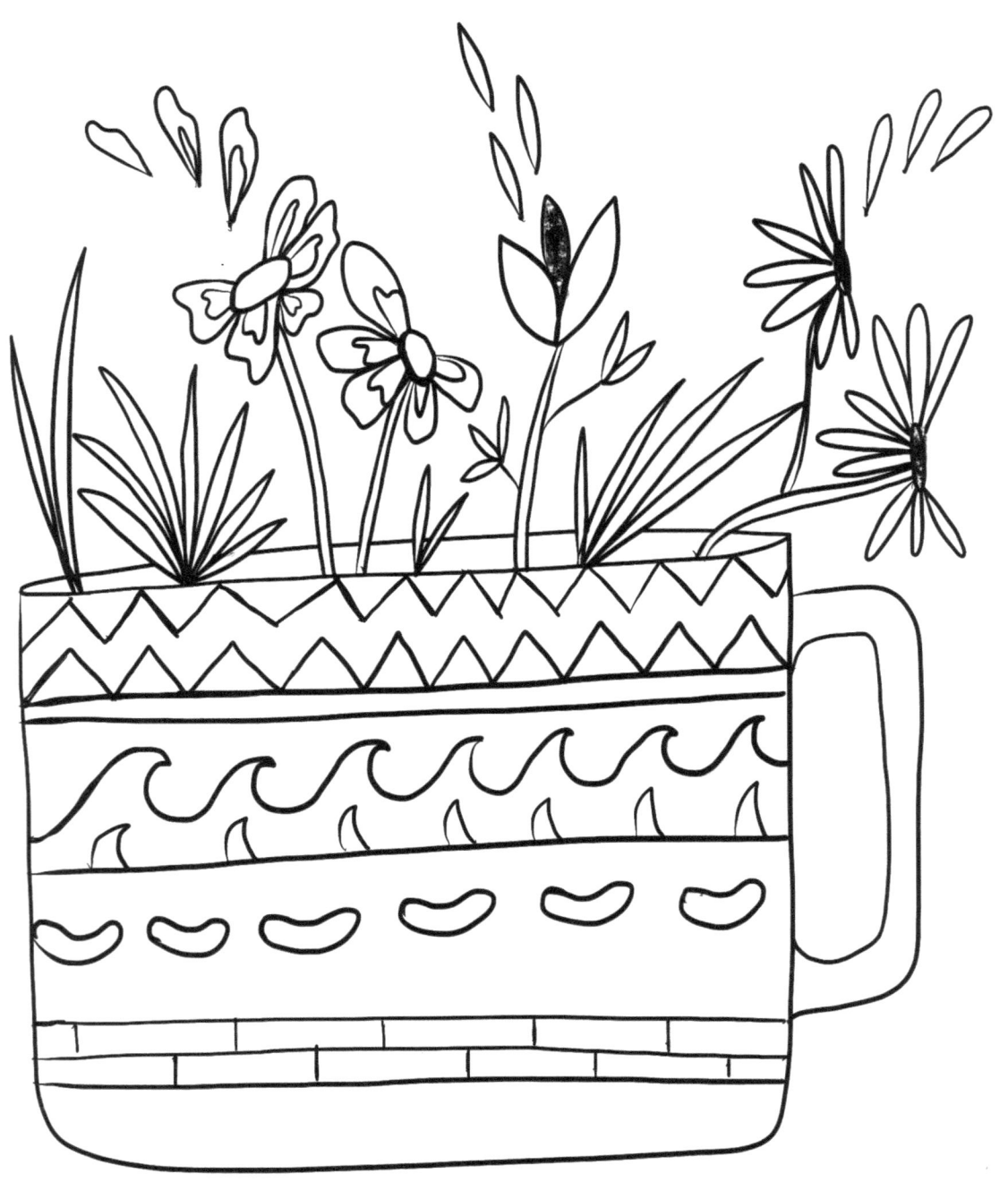

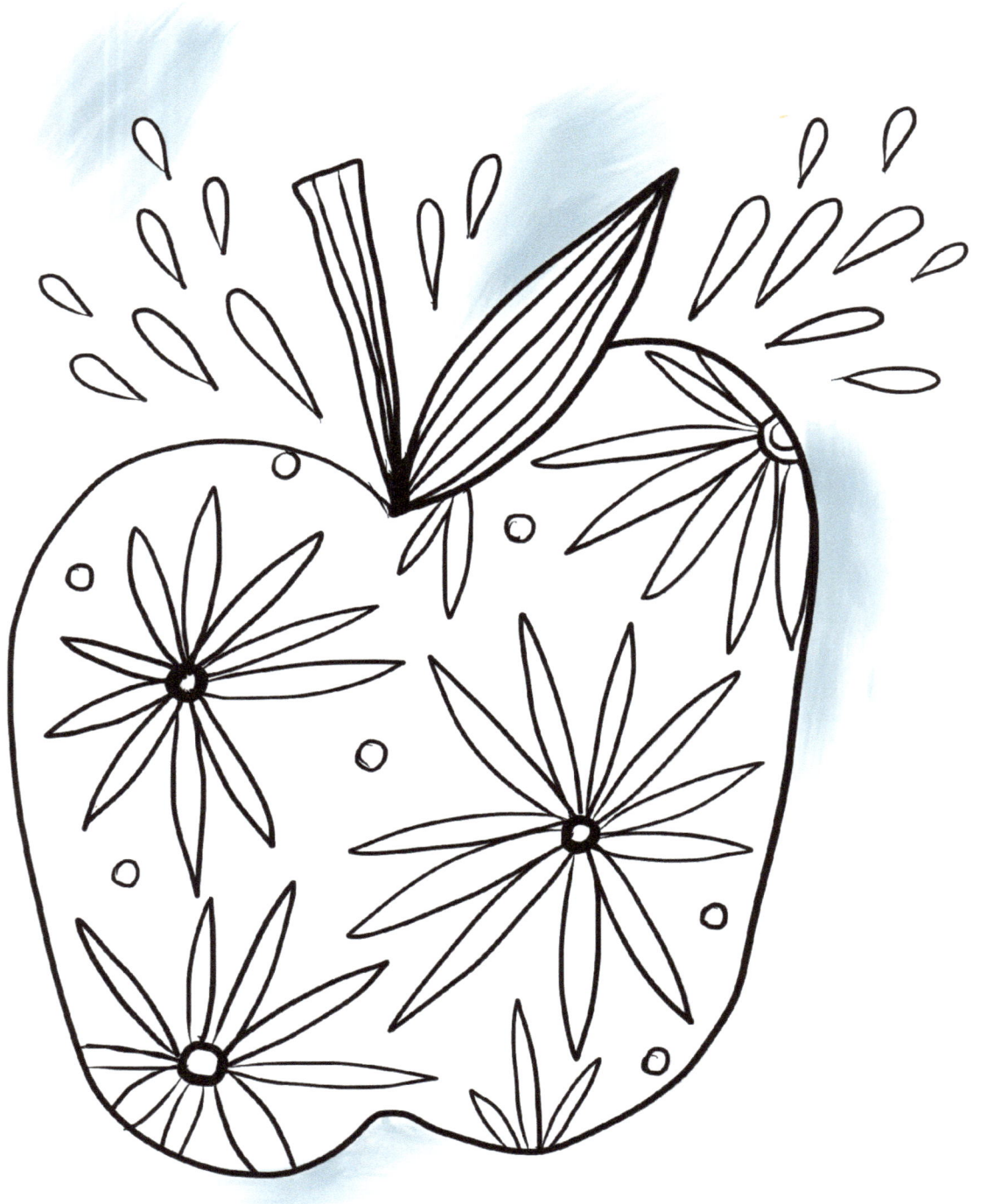

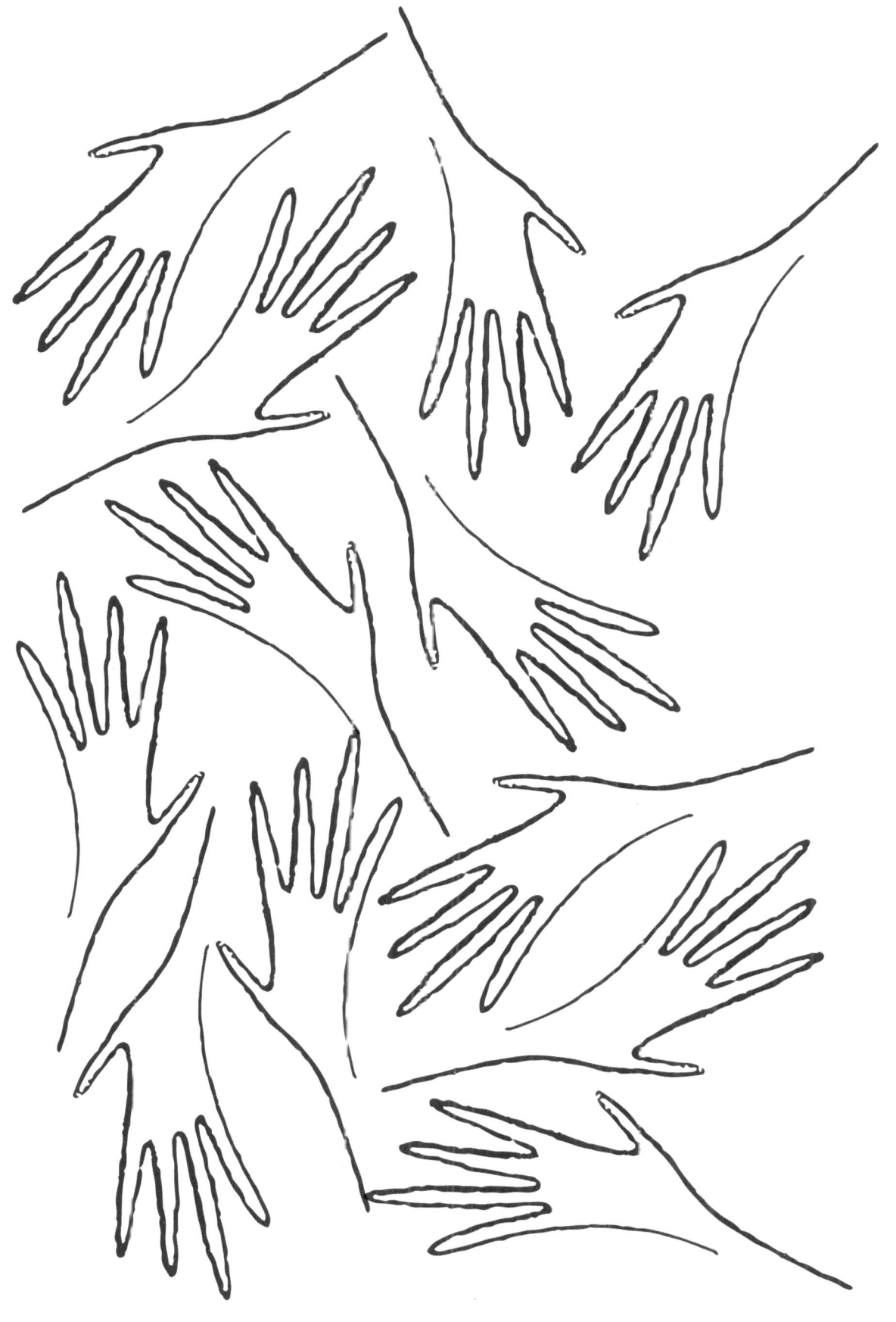

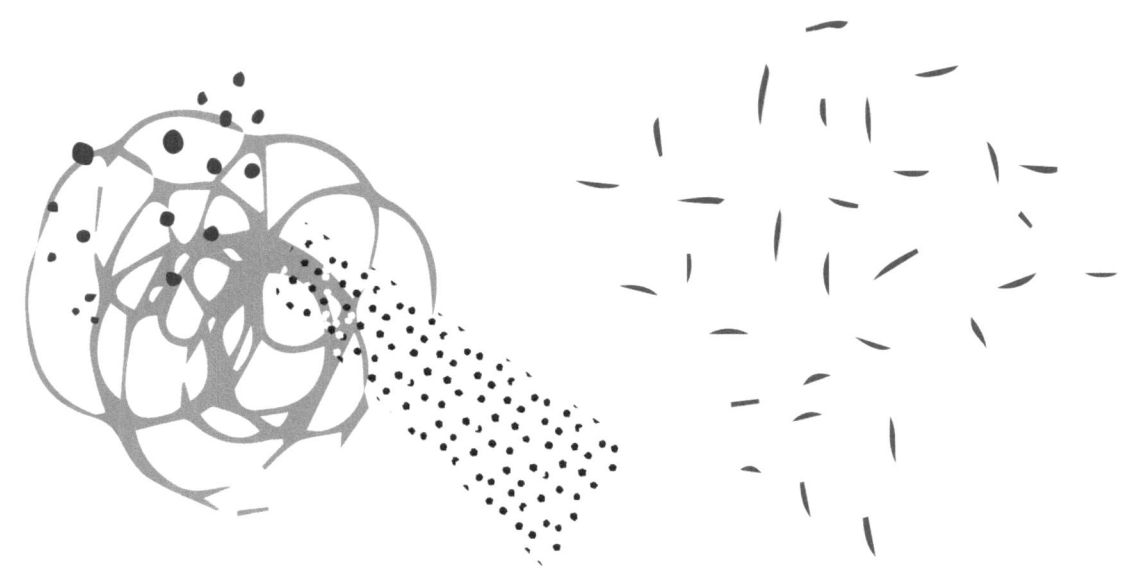

I ENCOURAGE YOU TO REVISIT EACH PAGE
AND FILL THE WHITE SPACE WITH
LINES OR DOTS OR DO DADS
AND WHATNOTS.

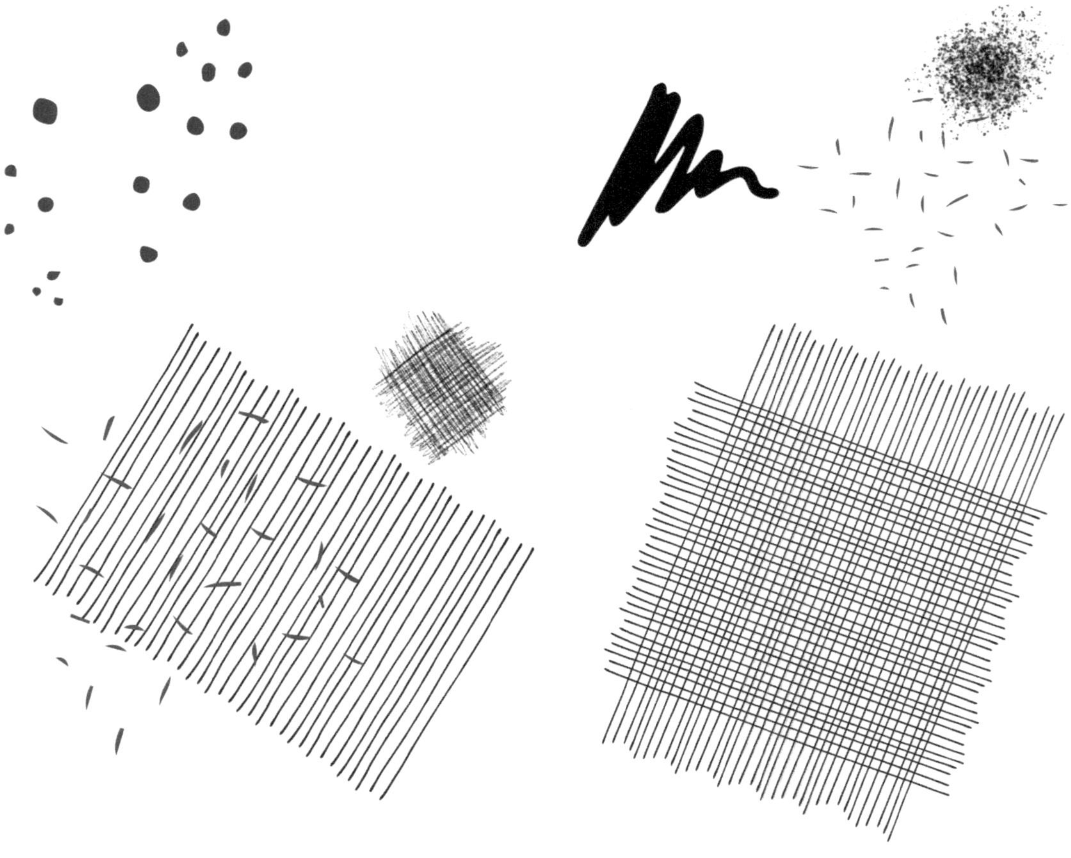

www.ingramcontent.com/pod-product-compliance
Lightning Source LLC
Chambersburg PA
CBHW050858180526
45159CB00007B/2712